LIVERPOOL CITY CENTRE

Architecture and Heritage

© A Moscardini 2011

Published by The Bluecoat Press, Liverpool.
Book design by MARCH Graphic Design Studio, Liverpool.
Printed in China by Latitude Press.

ISBN 9781904438 64 9

Front cover. Town Hall and Castle Street.

Tony Moscardini studied at the Glasgow School of Art, the
Glasgow School of Architecture and Urban Design at
Strathclyde University. He has worked in private practice, local
government, the New Towns and the Planning Inspectorate.

LIVERPOOL CITY CENTRE

Architecture and Heritage

An Urban Design Sketchbook

Anthony Moscardini

THE BLUECOAT PRESS

Contents

Introduction

This book does not set out to explain at length the historical growth of Liverpool, nor its architectural heritage, now commemorated in the City's award of World Heritage status, as this has been very well documented elsewhere. It is intended to be both a tribute and a warning. Unless the logic behind the City's form is understood, its character is in serious danger of being lost forever. Our major cities, of which Liverpool is one of the few with true international status, are in danger of losing their distinctive identity.

The identity threat has many causes: property speculation, the obsession with creating iconic buildings (for which a specific user can rarely be identified!) and the mantra of the development-led advocates who proclaim that the retention of valued historic buildings obstructs 'progress' and economic growth. Every building in an urban setting is an element in urban design. A tower building in its correct urban setting may accent its status and a special building can act as a focus. Plain buildings can act as modest background architecture although, as can be seen, this does not rule out innovative design.

Good architecture in urban design calls for good manners, and a good work is one among many companions, joined with them, but not striving to dominate or undermine them. One or two buildings may stand out as special pieces, the others acting as a background setting for them, but for most buildings, architectural humility is the basis of good urban design – the point being that it is possible to preserve and shape urban form. The townscape quality of an area often exceeds the value of its individual buildings.

It is a misconception that traditional buildings are intended to be solely the objects of isolated contemplation, but rather should be seen and experienced in relation to their settings. These unpretentious truths are being overlooked by a generation of developers who are obsessed with creating 'iconic' buildings which, by definition, unless strategically placed, set out to deliberately destroy the urban fabric.

In the urban design plan, buildings and their components have an identifiable scale, or module, and each city has its own. These can be characterised by the ratio of solid to void and their proportions. For example, the Liverpool 'module' has a clearly vertical scale. This is evident in the way individual facades have been knitted together in the outstanding urban spaces of Castle Street and Hope Street.

In the classic 1889 study *City Planning According to Artistic Principles* its author, Camillo Sitte, emphasises the significance of urban spaces in the heart of the city. He identifies basic layouts for public squares, approaches and avenues. The city is made up of 'rooms' and 'corridors' with a hierarchy of spatial types based on their size. In urban design these spaces vary from single intimate courts, to grand urban spaces.

A fundamental requirement of urban space is enclosure – it must be sufficiently enclosed on all sides so that attention focuses on the space as an entity. Enclosure can – as in an avenue – be on only two sides, forming a 'channel' in space.

Classic Public Squares

A building in space.

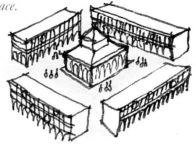

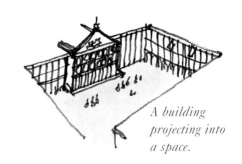

A building projecting into a space.

These are Camillo Sitte's classic public squares, as described in his 1889 study *City Planning in Accordance with Artistic Principles*. Examples of each can be found in present-day Liverpool.

A setting for a monument.

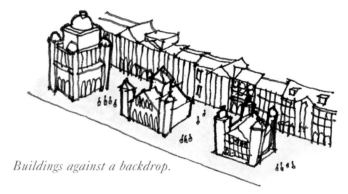

Buildings against a backdrop.

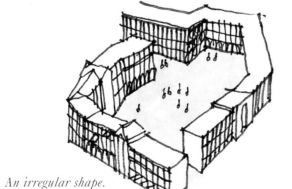

An irregular shape.

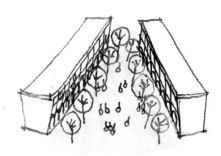

A channel of space.

The Urban Grain

The lines of historic streets, the building blocks, their massing and the predominant building vernacular, all combine to define the City's 'grain'. The plan shows that examples of each classic type of public-space vista and channel can be found in Liverpool city centre, and that buildings of status mark them – Hope Street and Castle Street being the prime examples. On a lesser scale, Bluecoat and Williamson Square are linked, whilst Pier Head and St John's Gardens provide the stage settings for remarkable world status buildings.

The urban designers of the new Paradise Street development have understood the need to develop in accordance with the 'grain'. By infilling alongside existing blocks, providing a background to Chevasse Park and creating a strong connection to Albert Dock, a new major linked space has been created.

The next part of this book is basically a Liverpool Sketch Book, with each area considered in detail to show where the illustrations fit into the urban scene. This book seeks to commemorate these buildings and enclosed spaces and, more importantly, bring them to the attention of the public at large.

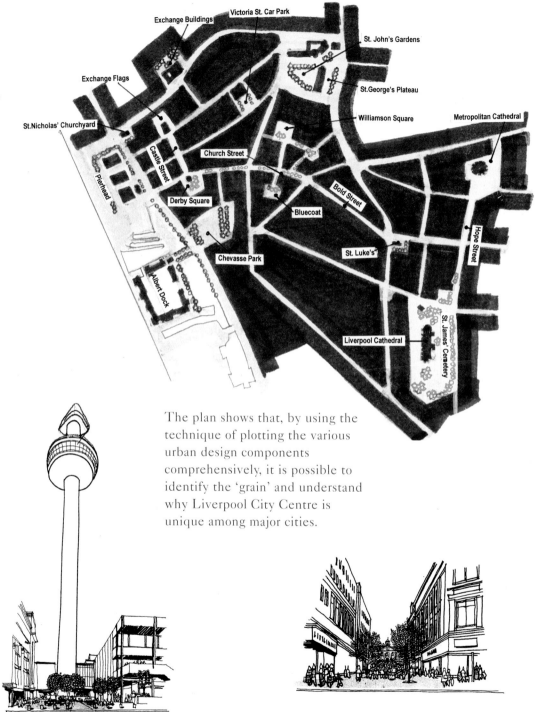

The plan shows that, by using the technique of plotting the various urban design components comprehensively, it is possible to identify the 'grain' and understand why Liverpool City Centre is unique among major cities.

Bold Street

Houghton Street

Church Alley

7

Around Pier Head

Liverpool's zenith was reached in the early part of the last century with the construction of the Pier Head group of commercial buildings. Liverpool is, without doubt, the foremost example of a city port in the United Kingdom and these buildings, best seen from the river, have given the city an international identity that stands comparison with other world ports.

The **Royal Liver Building,** designed by Aubrey Thomas, was the world's first multi-storey building with a reinforced concrete structure when it was erected (1908-1911). It was clearly influenced by the City's links with New York and has no counterpart in the UK. Built in a remarkably free and original style, its identifying features are the sculptural clock towers, surmounted by domes on which the mythical Liver Birds are perched.

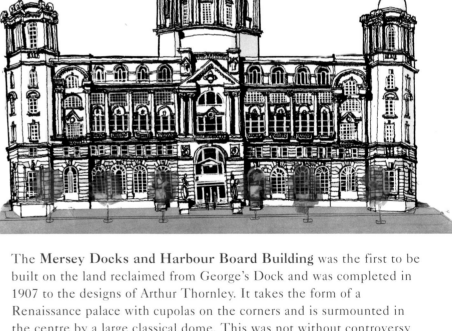

The **Cunard Building** dates from 1914 and was constructed during the First World War. The architects were Willink and Thicknesse, who designed it in the style of an Italian palazzo but with Greek revival detailing. The lesser of the three Pier Head buildings, it is nevertheless noteworthy for its good proportions and attention to detail. It is said that Willink's practice was given the commission because he regularly cycled to work alongside the chairman of the Cunard Company, from their homes in Fulwood Park!

The **Mersey Docks and Harbour Board Building** was the first to be built on the land reclaimed from George's Dock and was completed in 1907 to the designs of Arthur Thornley. It takes the form of a Renaissance palace with cupolas on the corners and is surmounted in the centre by a large classical dome. This was not without controversy at the time, since it is recorded that some members of the board questioned whether the additional cost of this feature could be justified simply to beautify the building! From his office in the top corner of the building, the chairman could survey the whole of his dockland empire.

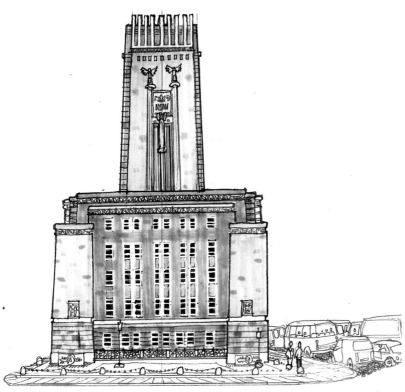

To the rear of the Pier Head Group is the landmark **George's Dock Building** housing the main ventilation shaft for the Mersey Tunnel. Completed in 1934, to the design of Herbert J. Rowse, the building was badly damaged during the Second World War and major rebuilding took place in the early 1950s. Although basically a classical building, its decoration is influenced by the modern movement. In its location, it serves the dual function of providing a point of reference on the ring road and a visual connection between the Pier Head Group and the building mass of the office area opposite.

The **Church of Our Lady and St Nicholas** is known as the Sailors' Church and can still be seen from the river. The Gothic Revival tower (1811), the oldest part of a much-rebuilt building, was designed by Thomas Harrison.

Pier Head, the Strand and Castle Street

Liverpool derives its unique character from the studied positioning of its landmark buildings. Starting from the streets running from the Pier Head, buildings have been sited in order to close views and change the direction of the grid.

The **White Star Building** (7) and **St Nicholas Church** (4) are not only part of the waterfront scene but also serve as markers for the city centre when approached from the ring road.

The **Town Hall** (5) projects into Dale Street at the point where it meets Castle Street. This is a classical town planning solution that effectively closes the view from Water Street and signposts the location of Castle Street.

The **Bank of England** (6), because of its formidable massing and its location directly on the axis of Brunswick Street, contains the view from the river and signals the mid-point of the Castle Street spine.

The **White Star Building** (1898), designed by Norman Shaw, was the first of a new generation of giant office blocks built in the city to meet the needs of the shipping trade.

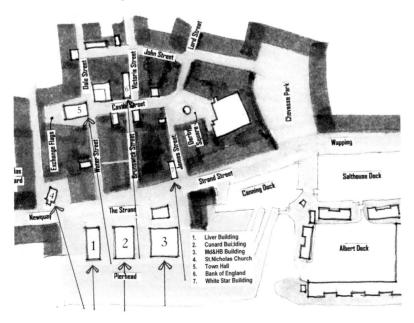

1. Liver Building
2. Cunard Building
3. Md&HB Building
4. St.Nicholas Church
5. Town Hall
6. Bank of England
7. White Star Building

The former **Bank of England** sits firmly on the axis of Brunswick Street.

Liverpool Town Hall projects into Water Street and presents its main facade on to Castle Street – sufficient to draw the eye to the next major component of the grid.

The Grade I Listed Buildings

Oriel Chambers is the most modern building in the city centre, although, unbelievably, it was built in 1864! Designed by a practically unknown Liverpool architect, Peter Ellis, it is one of the most significant buildings of its type in Europe. The building's controversial functional design aroused a great deal of controversy in its day and was described as 'an agglomeration of protruding plate glass bubbles'. Today, we appreciate the way it succeeds in being unique, whilst at the same time deferring to the general scale and proportion of its neighbours – a truly great example of good manners in urban design. The most dramatic approach to this building is through the India Buildings Arcade.

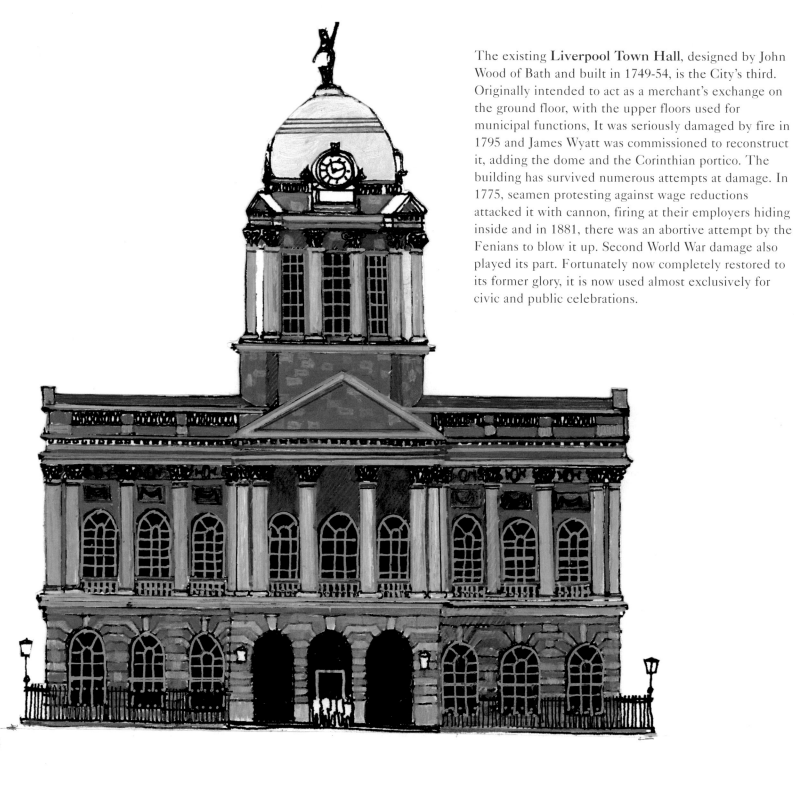

The existing **Liverpool Town Hall**, designed by John Wood of Bath and built in 1749-54, is the City's third. Originally intended to act as a merchant's exchange on the ground floor, with the upper floors used for municipal functions, It was seriously damaged by fire in 1795 and James Wyatt was commissioned to reconstruct it, adding the dome and the Corinthian portico. The building has survived numerous attempts at damage. In 1775, seamen protesting against wage reductions attacked it with cannon, firing at their employers hiding inside and in 1881, there was an abortive attempt by the Fenians to blow it up. Second World War damage also played its part. Fortunately now completely restored to its former glory, it is now used almost exclusively for civic and public celebrations.

Castle Street ~ the Commercial Heart of the City

Castle Street was the centre of banking activities at the zenith of the shipping trade. This has left a legacy of grand buildings, all of which have merged into a cohesive street of national significance. The street is terminated at either end by piazzas developed along classical lines.

The view looking towards the river. The **Town Hall** projects into the street and this is mirrored in the design of its neighbour **Martins Bank**. As with many views in the City, the Liver Birds oversee the scene, providing an instant point of location.

The **Town Hall** closes the view from Castle Street and the building facades, each building with its own identity, are, nevertheless, part of a unified whole. The arched openings to **Queen's Buildings** can be seen on the right. The Town Hall is an example of the classic urban design principle of setting a building in space in order to achieve maximum effect.

LIVERPOOL
TOWN HALL

Parr's Bank (1900), now Nat.West, is Norman Shaw's next building after the White Star Building and shows the same innovative use of banded materials.

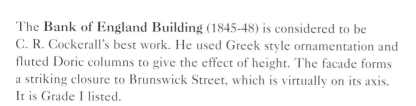

The **Bank of England Building** (1845-48) is considered to be C. R. Cockerall's best work. He used Greek style ornamentation and fluted Doric columns to give the effect of height. The facade forms a striking closure to Brunswick Street, which is virtually on its axis. It is Grade I listed.

Queen Buildings (1837-39) includes an arcaded approach to Castle Street which makes an ideal frame for **Parr's Bank**.

The **Adelphi Bank Building** closes the view from Victoria Street. Its siting fully justifies its eccentric unconventional design. W.F. Caroe was the architect and it was completed in 1892. It truly leaves its mark!

Castle Street ~ Two Interlinked City Squares

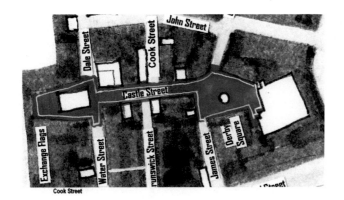

The potential for creating a grand piazza in this part of the city centre is apparent.

Castle Street looking towards the **Town Hall**. The **Equity and Law Building** (1970) designed by Quiggin and Gee, is clearly influenced by Oriel Chambers and fits comfortably into a street scene containing, among others, the **Bank of England Building** and **Queen's Buildings**. The Town Hall is fortunately not dwarfed by the background buildings.

Looking in the opposite direction, Derby Square houses the **Crown Courts** (1973) by Farmer and Dark, an example of the type of concrete panel exteriors in vogue at the time. The **Victoria Monument** (1902-05), probably the most ambitious of its kind, was designed by E. M. Simpson, then Professor of Architecture at Liverpool University and the large bronze sculptures are by Charles Allen, who was Vice Principal of the Liverpool School of Art.

Cook Street to Dale Street

The **Royal Insurance Building** (1897-1903) by Francis Doyle, a protege of Norman Shaw, who won a competition for its design. The Portland stone and granite exterior conceals a steel frame of advanced design, giving wide, column-free office areas. The sculptured frieze is the work of C. J. Allen and the gilded dome is a prominent landmark feature. Of note, also, is the way in which the adjoining more recent buildings defer to this architectural gem – a classical feature of urban design.

Melbourne Buildings (1854) is a narrow four storey building of stucco finish. It is a good example of how differing styles can be accommodated within the discipline of the ruling urban scale.

No. 16 Cook Street (1866) is the second and only other recorded building by Peter Ellis, the architect for Oriel Chambers. Built two years after that building, it is just as original with, in this instance, giant plate glass windows. Ellis seems to have paid the penalty for his unorthodox designs and is never after recorded as working as a civil engineer!

The **Prudential Building** (1885-86) by Alfred Waterhouse, built in his trademark red brick Gothic style. The building relies mainly on scale and rhythm for effect, rather than elaborate ornamentation. It is directly on the axis of Moorfields and thus fulfils its role as a landmark building.

23

Along Dale Street and Victoria Street

The **Municipal Buildings** (1862-68) were designed by John Weightman, Corporation Surveyor, and were built in a variety of styles culminating in a unique spire, which is a prominent feature on the city skyline.

The **Former Conservative Club** (1883), later the Municipal Annexe, was designed in the Renaissance style by Messrs F. and G. Holme, the winners of an architectural competition.

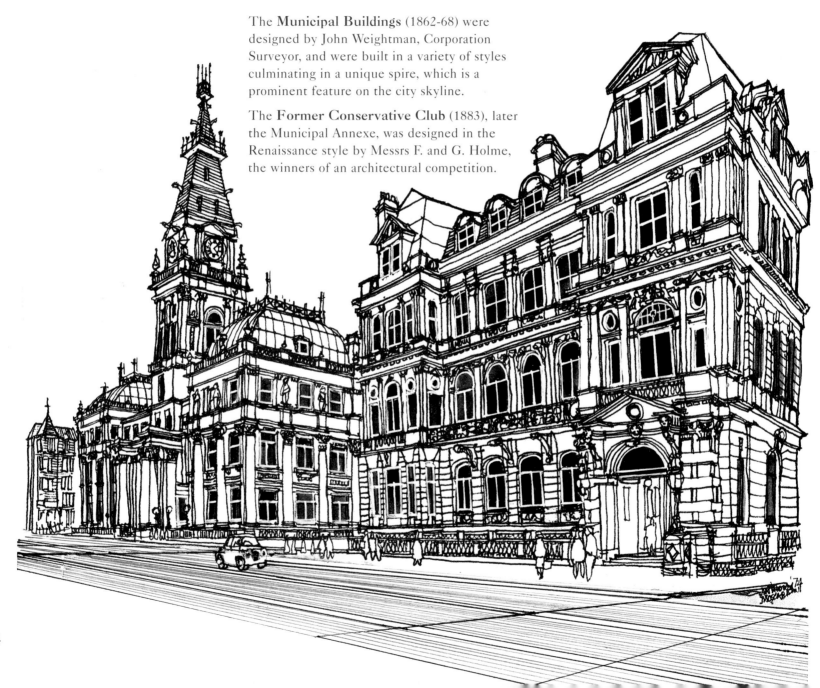

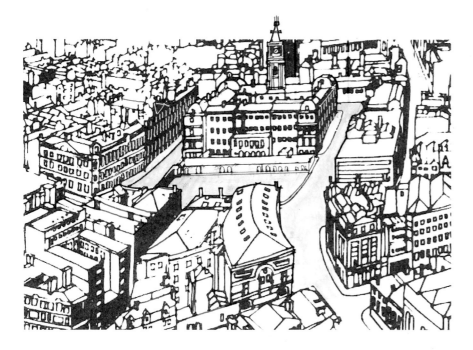

The Victoria Street Car Park, Liverpool's forgotten square. It is difficult to understand why the additional council accommodation, now sited elsewhere, could not have been used to make good the war-damaged rear elevation, giving a new entrance and facade looking on to a potential civic square.

The remains of the **General Post Office Building** (1894-99) have been incorporated into the modern shopping arcade that has been inserted into the shell of the old building. Although severely damaged in the Second World War, the sculptured entrance by E. Griffith survives, along with much of the Victoria Street frontage. In this way the new development has an entrance of quality and craftsmanship, the likes of which is neither affordable nor achievable in the present day.

The Conservation Centre, formerly the **Midland Goods Depot** (1872-74), was used to dispatch goods to and from the main railway depots. It is now used as a skills workshop for the restoration and repair of museum exhibits.

Williamson Square to Clayton Square

Built on the site of a music hall, the **Playhouse Theatre** was rebuilt as a repertory theatre in 1910/11 by S. D. Adshead, Professor of Civic Design at Liverpool University. The extension (1968), by Hall O'Donaghue and Wilson, is a model example of how to be progressive and also well mannered.

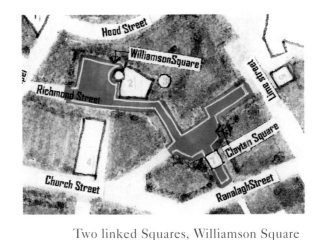

Two linked Squares, Williamson Square and Clayton Square

Clayton Square Shopping Arcade (1988) by architects Seymour Harris, is an arcade in the Victorian style. It is a focal point in the re-instated square and provides a visual link to Williamson Square.

Around Church Street

Some thirty years ago, Church Street was closed to vehicular traffic in order to create what was then the largest pedestrian precinct in the UK. This sketch, prepared at the time, showed how it could have looked. The scale of both the space created, and the buildings enclosing it, is that of a classic piazza. Only now, after years of cost cutting in the past, has a scheme materialised using the high quality paving materials the situation demands, if this unique shopping street is to reach its full potential as a city space.

The route to Bold Street passes Basnett Street. Note how the **Liverpool Playhouse Extension** projects forward of the building line, marking the location of Williamson Square. This urban design device is similar to the forward siting of the Town Hall marking Castle Street. Before Queens Square was redeveloped it was possible to glimpse the Museum through the gap.

The Liver Birds look over Church Street, locating it into the city grid. St John's Beacon is another point of reference.

29

Compton House (1867) is the key building on the street. Built to replace a fire-destroyed department store, it was, with typical Victorian efficiency, designed and built in just over eighteen months. Said to be a forerunner of many continental department stores, it continues in that use as a flagship Marks and Spencer store. It is directly on the axis with **Bluecoat Chambers**, forming, with Church Alley, a subsidiary square off Church Street.

Bluecoat Chambers, begun in 1716, is the oldest surviving building in the city centre. Built in the Queen Anne style, showing a Wren influence, the architect is not known. Originally built as a charity school, this use ceased in 1906, after which it was bought by Lord Leverhume to develop as an arts centre. This did not materialise, however, and in 1927 a group of enthusiasts formed the Bluecoat Society of Arts and proceeded to buy the chambers and have owned it since. The buildings were badly damaged during the Second World War but following successive rebuilding over the years, it is now probably in its best ever condition.

Bold Street to Lime Street

The **Lyceum** (1800-02) is (the last remaining building in Liverpool by Thomas Harrison of Chester. Originally built as a gentleman's club and to accommodate the Liverpool Library which, in 1757, was the first circulating library in Europe. It has had a number of uses since as a post office, building society and restaurant. It is a landmark building marking the entrance to Bold Street which, in turn, leads to another prominent landmark, **St Luke's Church**.

The **Cripp's Building** (1849) is an early Victorian example of a cast iron framed shop with two storeys of glass between slender iron columns. Built as a high-class ladies outfitters and drapers, it was so popular that, in 1861, *Fraser's Guide to Liverpool* noted that, 'The new premises, by their extent, tasteful arrangements and decorations, are ornamental, even in a town of commercial palaces'. Although 150 years later it is now a bookshop, the same comments still apply and in the era of the universal look-alike shop front, it survives as fresh and original as ever.

The **Adelphi Hotel's** landmark status is apparent from its position in relation to Ranelagh Street. The sketch, left, shows the hotel firmly marking one of the northern boundaries to the main shopping centre.

The Cases Street entrance to the **Clayton Square Arcade** is a small square with a number of buildings of significance including, right, the **Midland Hotel** (1900), which has many interesting features, notably Art Nouveau copper panels and ironwork. Adjoining, is the **Central Hotel**, inscribed 1675, and on the opposite corner is the **Abbey National Building** (1843) A classical stucco building, designed by William Culshaw.

The **Adelphi Hotel** (1912) was designed by Frank Atkinson, who also designed ships' interiors. This was appropriate, since the hotel was initially intended to cater for the flourishing passenger shipping trade across the Atlantic. Its prominent siting and classic appearance is a monument to that era. At that time it was owned by the Midland Railway Company and was considered to be the most prestigious hotel outside of London.

The Art Nouveau **Crown Hotel** (1905) is an important landmark building because of its position on the axis of Elliot Street.

St George's Hall and Environs

St George's Hall (1854) is the result of combining the outcome of two early competitions, for a Music Hall and an Assizes, both of which were won by 23-year-old architect, Harvey Lonsdale Elmes. As a result, he was commissioned to design the new building. Unfortunately, during construction in 1847, Elmes became ill and was advised to take a holiday in Jamaica where he died shortly after arrival. Professor C. R. Cockerell was appointed to carry on the work. After years of neglect, the Hall has been completely reinstated and can, once again, take its place in the life of the City.

St George's Plateau was reinstated in the 1970s using salvaged granite setts from slum clearance areas. It was a 'job creation' scheme using untrained labour, under the supervision of a traditional pavier, who had to be called out of retirement. The design is based on the Milton tile floor of the Concert Hall.

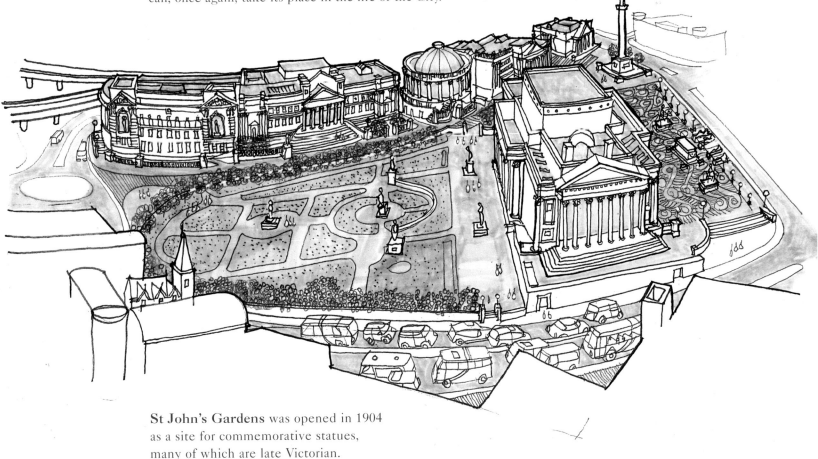

St John's Gardens was opened in 1904 as a site for commemorative statues, many of which are late Victorian.

William Brown Street

The former **College of Technology**, now a Museum Extension) designed by E. W. Mountford, was completed in 1902. Built in the Imperial style, it exhibits a wealth of sculpture by F. W. Pomeroy, who was also responsible for the bronze lamps on the impressive Byrom Street facade.

The **William Brown Library and Museum** (1860) was designed by competition winner, Thomas Allum, with modifications in order to reduce the cost, by Corporation Architect, John Weightman. The purpose of the building was to house the bequest of the Earl of Derby's Natural History Collection and the relocation of the Free Public Library in Duke Street. Because the Council could not meet the total cost, a wealthy merchant, William Brown, offered to defray the cost – an offer that was gratefully accepted!

The **Picton Reading Room** (1875) was designed by Cornelius Sherlock and was modelled on the Reading Room of the British Library. It provides a valuable civic design function, acting as a pivot where the street changes direction.

The **Walker Art Gallery** (1877) was designed by H. H. Vale with later extensions by Cornelius Sherlock and Sir Arnold Thornley. When he was elected Mayor in 1873, Alderman Andrew Barclay Walker, a local brewer, announced that he would meet the whole of the cost. The opening was observed as a public holiday in Liverpool.

Towards Hope Street

The former **Central Hall** (1905) designed by Bradshaw and Gass for the Liverpool Wesleyan Mission, in a variety of styles ranging from Byzantine to Art Nouveau. The addition of Gaudi-type decorated windows at street level seems strangely appropriate!

St Luke's Church designed in 1782 by John Foster Senior and eventually completed by his son, John Foster Junior, in 1831. Built in the Perpendicular Gothic style, it was severely damaged during the Second World War and remains as a monument to the blitz. The surviving west tower is a key landmark from all directions but is most dramatically seen in its view from Bold Street.

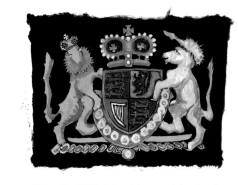

Detail of Kirkland's royal insignia.

The former **Kirkland's Bakery** still sports its royal links with Queen Victoria. Baking ceased in the 1970s and it became one of the earliest wine bars in the city.

Around Hope Street

Liverpool is unique in having two cathedrals, each in its own setting, linked by a street or channel, with the apt name Hope Street. The best approach is from Hardman Street, whose junction with Hope Street is at the midway point. The sketch (below) looks in the direction of the **Roman Catholic Cathedral**, built to the design of competition winner, Frederick Gibberd.

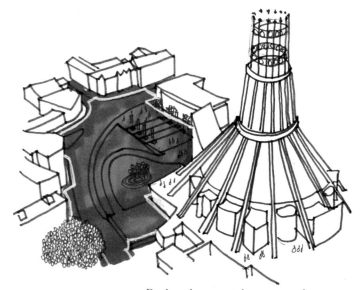

1. Roman Catholic Metropolitan Cathedral
2. Philharmonic Hall
3. Philharmonic Hotel
4. College of Art
5. Liverpool Cathedral
6. Kirkland's Bakery

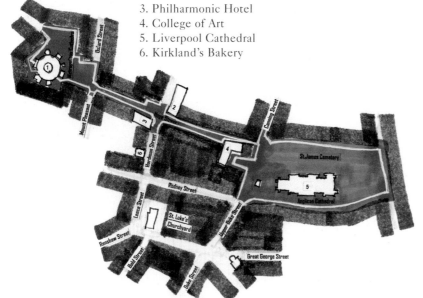

Redevelopment has created a worthy entrance piazza to the **Metropolitan Cathedral**. The relationship between the present building and the original **Crypt** can be readily seen.

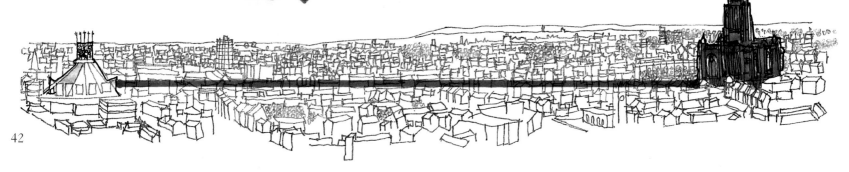

At the Metropolitan Cathedral

The **Metropolitan Cathedral of Christ the King** is a competition-winning design by the architect Frederick Gibberd and takes the place of Edwin Lutyens grand 1930 design for what, if built, would have been the second largest church in the world after St≠Peter's in Rome.

The great cathedral was started, but only the granite crypt, on which the present cathedral is built, was completed by the start of the Second World War.

In 1945, however, it was realised that the estimated cost, which had risen from £3m to £29m, was clearly unaffordable and the Church tried initially to scale down the cost of Lutyen's design to £4m by commissioning Adrian Scott, brother of Giles Gilbert, to prepare a much reduced scheme. This was widely criticised and dropped.

In 1960 a new Archbishop, John Heenan, launched a design competition for a cathedral that could be built within five years on a budget of £1m.

Gibberd was the winner, and the new cathedral was consecrated in 1967.

"The Greatest Church that never was." Edwin Lutyen's ambitious scheme envisaged major redevelopment of the area around the proposed church.

The **Philharmonic Hall** (1936-39) by Herbert J. Rowse, is strongly influenced by the severe brick Dutch style of the period. It nevertheless contains excellent examples of sculpture and etched glass in the Art Deco style.

ROYAL LIVERPO

PHILHARMONIC

ORCHESTRA

SUNDAY JUNE 8 AT
VLADIMIR ASHK
BRAHMS PIANO CONC
NO. 2
Pogramme includes:
Delius Paris, Song of a
Schubert Symphony No.
("The "Unfinished", com
fir t movements from Sch
le hated by Gerald Abr

40p from Philharmonic H
9 and Agents.

The **Philharmonic Hotel** is a magnificent Art Nouveau mixture, designed in 1900 by Walter Thomas. The rich gin palace interior is the result of the collaboration between Liverpool School of Art artists and craftsmen. Of particular note are the copper panels and ornamental gates by Bloomfield Bare.

The **College of Art Building**, commenced in 1882 by
Thomas Cook and continued in 1910 by Willink and
Thicknesse, is sited at right angles to Hope Street and
both closes the view at this end of the street and also
provides the enclosure for a mini piazza into which
setting has been placed an innovative piece of sculpture.
Created by John King, it is entitled *A Case History* and a
search will reveal that the cases belong to such worthies
as Arthur Askey, Paul McCartney and Charles Dickens.
Standing proud in the skyline is the tower of **Liverpool
Cathedral** leading the eye into the next major enclosed
open space in this part of the City.

At Liverpool Cathedral

The **Oratory** (1829), designed by John Foster in the form of a Greek Temple, was a mortuary chapel and marked the entrance to St James' Cemetery

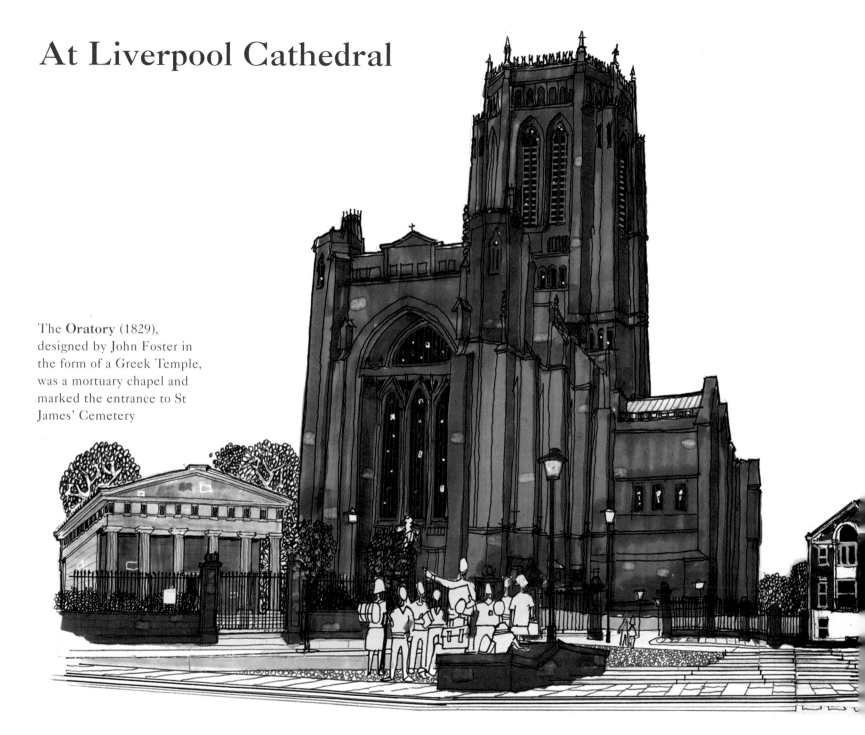

2004 saw the centenary of the laying of the foundation stone for **Liverpool Cathedral**. The design was chosen, controversially, by a national competition, initiated in 1901. On the basis of a small advertisement in the London newspapers, 103 portfolios were submitted, many of which were from the most famous architects of the day. Out of the final short list of six, Giles Gilbert Scott won, at the age of 23. Although he came from a distinguished architectural family, he had previously not designed any substantial building. His choice led to a great deal of controversy that was only resolved by appointing one of the assessors, G. F. Bodley, as joint architect. This was a stormy relationship, however, and was only concluded in 1907, when the elderly Bodley died and Scott became the sole architect. Gilbert Scott's winning design had, as its main feature, twin towers that were replaced in the 1910 revision by a massive central tower. Comparing the cathedral, as completed, inevitably leads to the conclusion that it bears little resemblance to the competition winner! In 1978, the year of completion, the cathedral received the RIBA Building of the Year award. The remainder of the St James' Mount site has not been short of controversy either, and was only ended when, on the basis of a proposal of the City Planning Officer (indirectly, in order to halt a scheme for municipal tenement housing on the site), the City Council agreed to make development of the land the subject of an architectural competition. A case of history repeating itself! As for the remainder of the site St James' Cemetery, after years of neglect, thanks to the valiant efforts of voluntary groups, it is well on the way to restoration to its former glory and there are moves to build a pedestrian bridge over it linking Gambier Terrace to the cathedral, as envisaged in Scott's original plan.

The **Dean Walter's Building** (1993), designed by Keith Scott, is part of John Moores University and a key part of the redevelopment of St James' Mount. It has resolved the requirements of its location, in that it provides a landmark at street level and closure to Rodney Street. Its sweeping curve leads the eye to the Cathedral entrance and its materials and proportions are in keeping with the Georgian facades of the adjoining area.

Two of the schemes not selected deserve special mention, since they represented pioneering design movements that are now seen as landmarks in twentieth century architecture and design.

The Art Nouveau Movement was represented by the iconic Glasgow architect Charles Rennie Mackintosh, whose imposing design featured his signature use of large areas of masonry balanced with innovative use of glass windows decorated with floral tracery.

Scott's design was radically revised twice – first in 1910 and later, in 1967, when stone had increased to twelve times its 1904 cost, and bears no resemblance to the winning scheme. Ironically, it is closer in many ways to that of Mackintosh!

William Richard Lethaby, a pupil of Norman Shaw and a disciple of William Morris, led a team of like-minded associates, sculptors and architects in the Arts and Crafts Movement to submit a design featuring a series of folded concrete vaults. Small side chapels also functioned as buttresses, with the whole composition dominated by a tapering detached campanile.

The double fronted house, **No. 60 Hope Street** (early nineteenth century) displays all the best features of housing design at that time. Of note is the ornamental fan light over the main doorway.

No. 59 Rodney Street is a Grade II Georgian house and is typical of the terrace housing that makes up most of this street and the surrounding area. It is, in its entirety, a landmark area. The house itself is notable as the former dwelling and studio of the eminent photographer, Edward Chambre Hardman, and is now in the care of The National Trust.

Around Duke Street

Designed by Joseph Franklin, successor to John Foster Junior as Corporation Surveyor, the former **Congregational Church** (1841) is a landmark classical stone building with a semi-circular drum porch, surmounted by a circular dome held on giant order Corinthian columns. It closes the view from Berry Street and links to **St Luke's Church**, forming a linked channel in this part of the city centre.

The distinctive **Chinese Arch** (2000) is a millennium gift from China. It is a gateway to the traditional Chinese quarter and commemorates the City's long association with that nation.

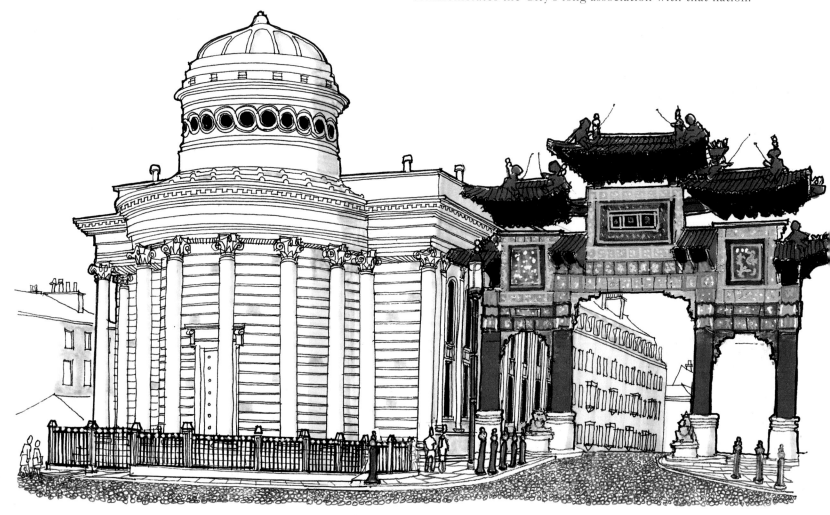

Church House (1884) designed by Edward Grayson, was originally built as premises for the Mersey Mission to Seamen. Its fine terracotta and brick facade and its location, closing the view from Duke Street, makes it uniquely suited to act as a landmark building.

The **Royal Institution** was built originally as a house and business premises for Thomas Parr, an important Liverpool banker in about 1799. The Royal Institution for the encouragement of literature, science and the arts, was founded by William Roscoe and the house was converted in 1817 by William Aitken, who added the Greek Doric porch. The Institution was incorporated by Royal Charter in 1822 and continued, until recently, in educational use as the University Extra Mural Department.

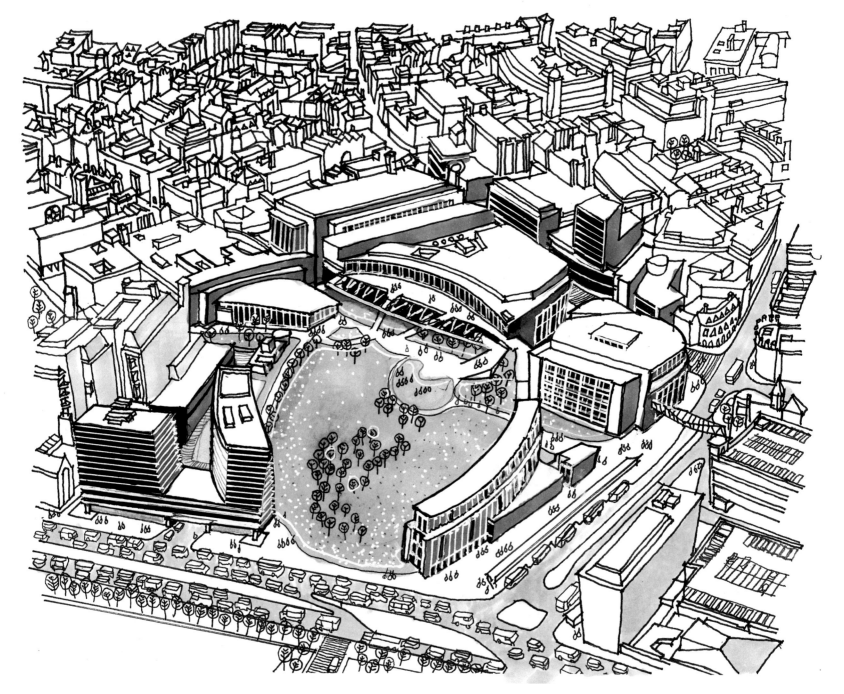

Liverpool One

Reputed to be Europe's largest retail development, this scheme is a combination of infill development that respects the historic city centre grain, and redevelopment around the existing **Chevasse Park**, itself a proposal implemented from an earlier city centre plan.

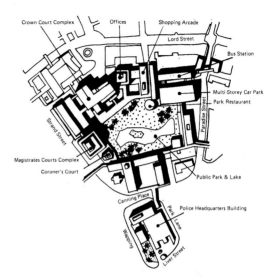

The scheme is an excellent example of the use of buildings primarily to create enclosure, while at the same time allowing scope for individual building design. Galleries and viewing platforms are deliberately aligned to anchor the development to traditional landmark buildings and give views over the Waterfront.

The end result is a fine example of contemporary urban design based on historic design principles.

Chevasse Park, and the buildings enclosing it, is the 'hub for the central retail area. The designers have recognised the need to knit the new with the old by creating new links and views that reinforce the city grain.

History The model (right) shows the proposal for the Paradise Street site as shown in the City Centre Plan of 1965, the land having been left in its undeveloped state since the blitz of 1941.

The proposal, for a bus station at ground level, with several floors of car parking surmounted by five 18-storey tower blocks, was extremely complex and no developer could be found who was able to raise the funds to implement the scheme. It is interesting to note that, apart from the architectural interpretation, the concept of using buildings to create a new city space (in this case a park) was established even then.

The Plan of 1968 shows the same urban design concept but with the uses housed in separate units, in order to meet development costs viable at the time. Although it did not produce 'iconic' architecture the site housed a bus station and multi-storey car park, a hotel, offices, a fire station and flatted factories that served the city centre well for many years.

As can be seen, the urban design principles for this part of the City have remained remarkably consistent. The site has now been developed to its full potential as the city hub envisaged over 40 years ago. Those who castigate the planners for lack of achievement, might best turn their attention to those who, throughout the time, were unable to create the economic climate so favourable to today's regeneration.

Under the 1968 Plan for the Strand/Paradise Street area, the comprehensive development area provided sites for the Crown Courts and County Police Headquarters, to be followed later by a new Magistrates Court. The model, below, is consistent with the 2008 Liverpool One scheme.

Inside Liverpool One

Liverpool One comprising thirty new buildings and a public park has revitalised the City Centre by creating an urban landscape firmly locked into the city grain. In the best urban design tradition, interesting new city spaces have been devised, existing ground levels have been exploited and vistas terminated by historic landmark buildings.

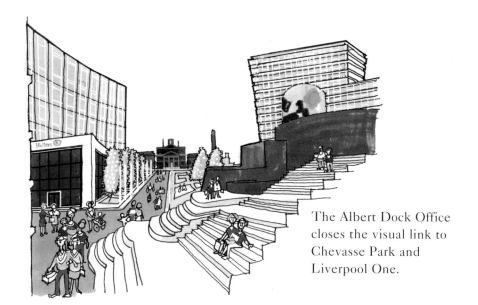

The Albert Dock Office closes the visual link to Chevasse Park and Liverpool One.

The main shopping street is anchored to the gilt dome of the Royal Insurance building.

Keys Court is an award-winning arcade providing a contemporary solution to a traditional urban design shopping street.

Around the Albert Dock

The **Dock Traffic Office** (1841-45) is a Grade I listed building designed by Philip Hardwick, with the top storey added by Jesse Hartley in 1848. The building is exceptional in that it takes the form of a classical temple but uses brick and cast iron for its construction. The building marks the main approach to the **Albert Dock** complex.

Built between 1841-45, the five-storey warehouses around the **Albert Dock** were also designed by Philip Hardwick and Jesse Hartley. They enclose a courtyard of giant proportions, whose effect is doubled by reflections on the enclosed water. The grand scale, the uncompromising simplicity of design and the quality of the materials used – brick, granite and cast iron – uniquely in the form of Doric columns – all add to the majesty of this group. Note the visual link to **Liverpool Cathedral**.

In the early 1970s, the **Albert Dock Buildings** were left unoccupied and virtually abandoned by the Dock Company. The dock system was left open to the river and quickly silted up to the extent that it was thought that the buildings would become unstable. In 1975, a proposal was put forward by the then Liverpool Polytechnic (now John Moores University) based on a scheme prepared by the Head of Architecture, Ken Martin, that the dock buildings be used to house new premises for the Polytechnic. At the same time, ideas were being promoted by Liverpool Museum for a maritime museum in one of the buildings. Unfortunately, the City Council could not raise its share of the funds and the project was abandoned. Ironically, a structural survey prepared as part of the proposals, proved that the replacement of water with silt in the dock had had no detrimental affect on the timber pile foundations of the warehouses. The sketches (over leaf), show how the scheme might look, were part of a presentation to the Council at that time. In 1981, the Merseyside Development Corporation was set up with the specific task of regenerating the dock areas. The result was to attract commercial and residential uses, and, most notably the Maritime Museum and the Tate Liverpool. As a result, it is today one of the top visitor attractions in the country.

The Museum of Liverpool 2011
It opened the day the Royal Liver Building celebrated its centenary.

Back to Pierhead

An era of unprecedented availability of funds through grants and record borrowing has produced a great deal of 'regeneration' in the City Centre. Much of this has fitted into the urban fabric and rejuvenated many buildings of merit. The overwhelming urge to produce 'iconic' buildings is always evident, nowhere more so than Pierhead. The public will judge for itself the merit of the new additions to the scene. Suffice to say that they have little architectural integrity with their neighbours in terms of scale, nor do they provide 'community gain' by way of creating enclosed space or the retention of historic views. All that can be said is that they provide contrast and only confirm how impressive the Pierhead group and the adjoining Albert Dock really are.

The new building leads the eye to its more ornate neighbour.

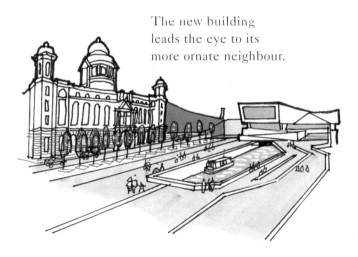

For all the regeneration projects, the Pierhead is the image the eye settles on. It represents history, the monument to a great age of shipping prosperity, the new age of tourism and the appreciation of great urban design. It is difficult to imagine any of today's new buildings aiming at a life of 100 years let alone eternity.

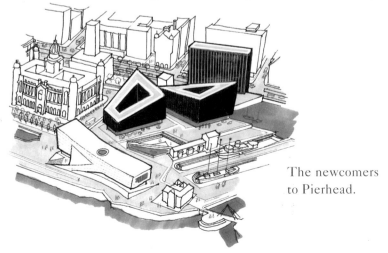

The newcomers to Pierhead.

Squares and Channels

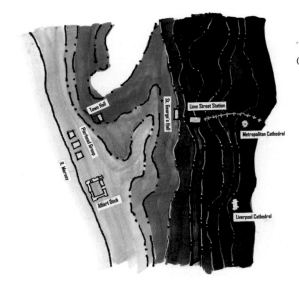

Topography. Liverpool City Centre showing contours

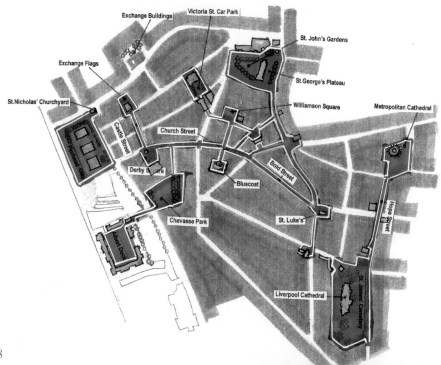

A study of the plan of Liverpool city centre shows that historic urban design principles have been understood and applied in practice. Examples of all the classic public square types are represented and have provided a strong framework for growth over the last two centuries. Cities have their own special character, which derives from their topography and their relationship to lines of communication. Some cities, for example Edinburgh and Bath, have developed on the basis of a grid-iron regular plan, but central Liverpool lies in a shallow basin, precluding an urban pattern of this kind. The business and commercial sector is situated at the centre of the basin and is built around a small depression that was once the old 'Pool', breaking out to the waterfront at the Pier Head. The eighteenth century Town Hall, because of its siting at a high point, is a pivot marking the division between the inner centre and the waterfront. The view along Dale Street and Water Street, framed by walls of buildings of majestic scale and closed by the Waterfront buildings, is one of the most impressive in the City.

Inland, the land rises to a ridge of low hills, on which the two cathedrals are sited. St George's Plateau, on the level of Lime Street, houses a gathering of cultural buildings notably St George's Hall and the William Brown Street Group of Museums, Library and Art Gallery. Throughout the older parts of the central area there is a unity of architectural scale and robust materials that give the City its unique maritime character.

An Urban Grid

This plan shows the landmark buildings plotted on the city centre plan. A combination of this plan with the two on the preceding page gives a picture of the City Centre's urban form against which future development can be evaluated.

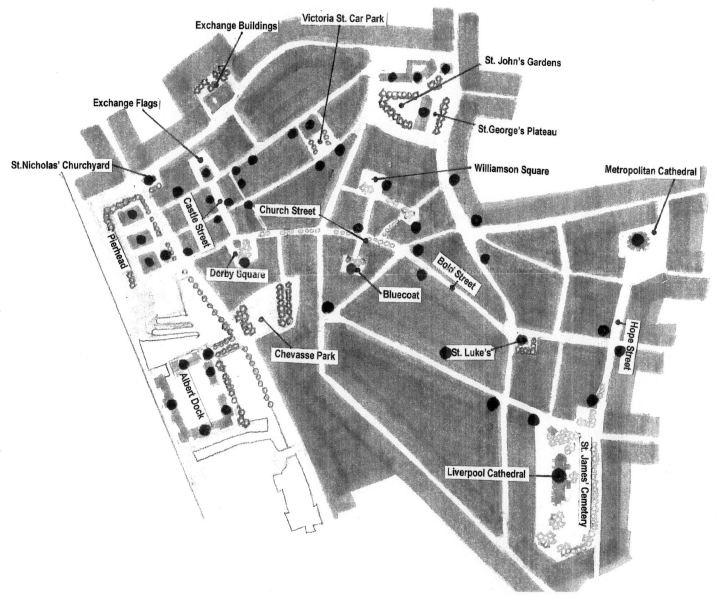

Exchange Buildings

Victoria St. Car Park

St. John's Gardens

Exchange Flags

St. George's Plateau

St. Nicholas' Churchyard

Williamson Square

Metropolitan Cathedral

Castle Street

Church Street

Pierhead

Derby Square

Bold Street

Bluecoat

Hope Street

Albert Dock

Chevasse Park

St. Luke's

St. James' Cemetery

Liverpool Cathedral

Landmark Buildings

Individual buildings play an important role in the total cityscape. A distinctive facade or dome can be a fine vista termination, either at the end of a street, or on the skyline. It is apparent, looking at the grid of landmark buildings, that the City's urban form has developed over a long period, in accordance with historic planning principles. This plan looks at many of the most significant buildings, and plots the way they contribute to the tapestry that is individual to Liverpool.

Those who say that 'planning' hinders city development, should look at the history of the great cities, of which Liverpool is one, and examine the way they have developed. Even in comparatively recent times it is no accident that, for example, the Town Hall has been 'twinned' with the Crown Courts, creating the long piazza of Castle Street, with prominent buildings at its ends.

Landmark buildings tell us where things begin and end, and they signpost important hubs. They are the fixed points in a constantly changing scene and give a consistency to the objectives of urban design. It is not possible to plot the total of the many weaves that comprise the complete tapestry that makes Liverpool city centre unique, and it adds to the experience to walk around the streets and spot the many more landmarks than are recorded here.

This book will have achieved its purpose if:

• It has helped those who admire the city centre to understand how it has evolved into the urban form that gives Liverpool its 'world class' attraction.

• It has shown that it is possible to identify an urban grid made up of landmark buildings, squares, channels and vistas, that gives the city centre its unique character and provides the framework against which new development should be measured.

• It succeeds in bringing to the attention of the public at large, those buildings and town planning features that make up the distinctive character of the centre.

• It helps members of the public to participate in the often Byzantine and obscure debates when new developments (hardly ever shown in the context of the larger area) are foisted upon them in the name of 'progress'. It is important to remember that public participation in the planning process is a basic right, enshrined in legislation, and all those who care about the City are entitled to have their views heard.

Visionary plans can damage the health of the city

Urban design is about surgery not butchery. The model of the 1946 Reconstruction Plan shows in retrospect how unrealistic it is to attempt to put forward visions of the future. For example, the plan shows a grand new passenger terminus and four more replica office blocks on Pierhead. In reality, the transatlantic passenger trade had disappeared within five years and not much later, shipping operations had moved to the north docks.

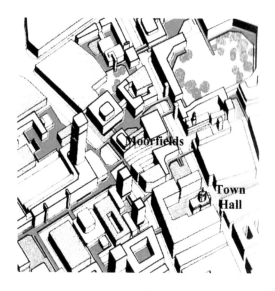

The 1965 Plan proposed the redevelopment of Moorfields. Within five years it had been designated a Conservation Area and is now part of the World Heritage Site. In truth, long term 'visions' only distort the planning system and create 'planning blight' which hinders the improvement of areas and the re-use of heritage buildings.

Illustrations

Urban design, unlike conventional town planning (which nowadays appears to be restricted to 'flat earth' land use zoning and written policies), is based on an understanding of the built structure and its relationship to topography.

Liverpool, as seen from the waterfront, is in the champions' league of world cities and it is important to study the reason for this.

Cartoonists see it as part of their art to take a subject and focus on its main characteristics and these immediately register in the mind. Those who admire Liverpool have their own particular vision of the city and it is certain that changing its character is not part of it!

The drawing on this page is my attempt to capture the character and spirit of the city centre. In my mind, it tells more about Liverpool than any number of coloured plans.